GLOBAL **HERB** MANUAL

By Zeke Fortisevn

AN HERBAL GIFT

to

BETTER HEALTH

and

HAPPINESS

Global Health Ltd.
Box 18, Site 1, RR2
Tofield, Alberta, Canada
T0B-4J0

First and second printings, 1988
Third printing, 1989

Printed in U.S.A.

HERBAL HEALING

Welcome to the wonderful world of herbal healing. It is a discipline which is making a comeback after several decades of almost dormancy on our continent.

Dating back to prehistoric times, herbalism is one of the oldest forms of healing. A prescription found written on a 4000-year-old Sumerian tablet called for myrrh and white willow. Those herbs can still be found in health food stores today. Hippocrates spoke of the virtues of white willow. The Bible, Egyptian hieroglyphics and ancient Chinese writing all refer to herbs as medicine.

Most of the herbs in this book have a very long history of use. It is therefore safe to say that most of the herbs in this book have been tested on millions of people over hundreds (and sometimes thousands) of years.

Programs to restore and maintain the body's health should include diet and exercise as well as herbal foods. To begin an herbal program, it is usually best to start building up the digestive system. Then nutrients can be more efficiently absorbed (see index under "digestion," "three day cleanse" and "lower bowel cleanser") and subsequent self-heal programs will be more effective.

This booklet is a short overview of God's pharmacy. After you read it, I encourage you to study some of the more advanced herbal books. They will go into more depth about how you can be helped by the absolutely fascinating study of herbal medicine.

TABLE OF CONTENTS

SINGLE HERBS.. 5

HERBAL COMBINATIONS...21

HERBAL EXTRACTS, OILS and OINTMENTS..........42

HERBAL SYRUPS...47

GLOSSARY...49

DIETS...53

BIBLIOGRAPHY...58

INDEX...59

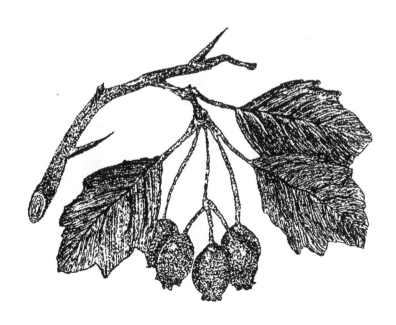

SINGLE HERBS

ACTIVATED CHARCOAL

Activated charcoal relieves intestinal gas and discomfort. It is used for emergency relief from poisoning when vomiting should not be induced. Each particle of activated charcoal contains many small chambers and cavities which will bind up unwanted toxins and gasses from the stomach and intestines. They are then taken safely through the digestive system. CAUTION: Activated Charcoal may absorb vitamins and prescription drugs. It should therefore not be used within 2 hours of taking medication.

ALFALFA

Alterative, nutritive. Alfalfa is an excellent blood purifier and is therefore used for arthritis. It aids in the assimilation of protein, fats and carbohydrates. Alfalfa is very high in trace minerals.
Alfa-Max is a highly concentrated (10x) extract in which alfalfa is made more assimilable by removal of the indigestible cellulose fiber.

ASTRALAGUS

Tonic. Astralagus works with the white blood cells to help fight infection. It helps build up the immune system.

BARLEY GRASS

Cell proliferant, internal deodorant, tonic for immune system, mild appetite suppressant. Barley grass is an excellent source of chlorophyll and has high levels of beta-carotene, Vitamins B1, B2 and B6, folic acid and choline. Each of these six nutrients helps to build up the immune system. Barley grass gives relief to fevers, diarrhea and stomach irritations. It speeds up regeneration of healthy tissue. This means, for example, that wounds and burns will heal quicker. In a weight loss program, take 2 or 3 capsules 3 times daily with a large glass of water. Barley grass is an excellent source of live enzymes. (See glossary under "enzymes" for more information.)

BAYBERRY

Astringent. Bayberry may be used in all mucus membrane conditions and for inflammation and infection of the bowels. Historically people have used the powdered herb as snuff for nasal catarrh.

BEE POLLEN

Blood builder. Bee pollen is one of the richest and most perfect foods in nature. It is often used by athletes to give them extra stamina and energy. Bee pollen is rich in vitamins, trace minerals and amino acids. It has natural interferon and therefore helps to build the immune system.
CAUTION: Some people may be allergic to bee pollen. To test it out, dissolve a small amount under the tongue. If eyes water and nose runs, do not use.

BEET POWDER

Beet powder is one of the best-known plant sources of assimilable iron. It is valuable for liver and gall bladder and contains Vitamins A,B and C, sodium, potassium, calcium and chlorine.

BLACK WALNUT

Anti-fungal, antiseptic, astringent, vermifuge. In capsule form black walnut is used against internal parasites. It is best to take one to three capsules daily at mealtimes. In extract form, black walnut is used for ringworm and other skin disorders. (See Black Walnut Extract in Herbal Extracts section.)

BLACK COHOSH

Antispasmodic, emmenagogue. Black cohosh is a natural precursor to estrogen. Native American women used it for female complaints, pelvic conditions, uterine troubles and menstrual cycles. It helps relieve premenstrual and menstrual cramps and is also helpful in relieving pain and inflammation. CAUTION: Dosage should not exceed four capsules per day. Overdosage can cause vertigo and nerve center irritation. Black cohosh should not be used in early stages of pregnancy.

BLESSED THISTLE

Emmenagogue, galactagogue, stomachic, tonic. Blessed thistle increases milk while nursing, balances hormones and helps with cramps, irregular menstrual cycles and other female problems. It is used for anorexia and sluggish digestion.
CAUTION: Should not be taken in large amounts during pregnancy.
NOTE: Black cohosh is better than blessed thistle for hormone imbalances.

BUCHU

Diuretic, stimulant, antiseptic for the urinary tract. Buchu is used for chronic inflammation of the bladder, irritation of the urethra, urine retention, nephritis, cystitis and catarrh of the bladder. It is one of the most efficient remedies for urinary and prostatic infections.
NOTE: ANY diuretic will leach potassium from the system. It is therefore a good idea to take a natural source of potassium such as dandelion root in the event that a person is taking a diuretic EVERY day for over a month.

BURDOCK

Alterative, diaphoretic, diuretic. Burdock is one of the best blood purifiers for chronic infection, arthritis, rheumatism, skin diseases (including eczema) and sciatica. It clears kidneys of excess wastes and uric acid by increasing the flow of urine and is therefore excellent for gout. Burdock has been known to reduce swelling and deposits within joints and knuckles of arthritis sufferers. Because it has digestive enzymes and bile stimulants, burdock will cause the body to secrete gas and will help eliminate the putrefying factor in the intestines.

CAUTION: It is not advisable to detoxify the blood too quickly. It is safer to start with one capsule twice daily and build up to two capsules three times daily over a three week period.

BUTCHERS' BROOM

Vasoconstrictive. Improves venous circulation. Butchers' broom builds up the structure of the veins. It is therefore used for hemorrhoids and other types of varicose veins. Healing of varicose veins will be faster when butchers' broom is combined with Red Clover Combination (two of each daily produced excellent results.)

CAUTION: Should not be used in cases of high blood pressure.

CASCARA SAGRADA

Hepatic, gentle laxative. Cascara sagrada is one of the most valuable remedies for chronic constipation.

CAUTION: Prolonged use of this or any other laxative should be avoided.

CATNIP

Carminative, diaphoretic, sedative. Catnip eases colic. It is a digestive tonic. Catnip is sometimes mixed with fennel in tincture form for colic. (See Catnip & Fennel Extract in the index.)

CAYENNE

Carminative, stimulant, diaphoretic. Cayenne stimulates circulation, increasing pulse rate and strengthening it. It is useful in colds, sinus problems and many respiratory ailments. As an emergency treatment for shock, drinking warm water with one to three teaspoons of cayenne powder can be expected to relieve shock immediately. Cayenne is excellent for hemorrhage. Powder can be poured directly onto wound to immediately stop bleeding. Using one capsule three times daily with water or juice is a good tonic for heart and circulation. This latter routine is followed 4 days per week.
CAUTION: Should not be used in cases of hyperacidity.

CHAMOMILE

Emmenagogue, nervine, sedative, digestive aid. Chamomile is used for insomnia, nervousness, weak stomachs and to stimulate appetite.

CHAPARRAL

Alterative (with cleansing concentrating on liver and kidneys), antibiotic, antiseptic, anti-oxidant, parasiticide. Chaparral is one of nature's best antibiotics. It is good for treating bacterial, viral and parasitic infections. CAUTION: Because of the strong cleansing action, dosage should start small (one capsule twice daily) and built up slowly over a three week period (to two capsules three times daily.)

CHICKWEED

Antipyretic, blood builder, demulcent, mild appetite suppressant. It is used for skin irritations such as boils, acne, rashes and eczema.

CHLORELLA

Highest-known source of natural chlorophyll. Chlorella is effective in detoxifying the liver and bloodstream, in cleansing the bowel and feeding friendly bowel flora. It helps the body absorb iron. In one study, using 1416 men taking the equivalent of six capsules daily, chlorella greatly increased body's resistance to cold viruses. In another Japanese study, it accelerated the healing of serious wounds. When taken with prescribed medication, chlorella hastens the healing of peptic and duodenal ulcers and gastritis. One study with tumor-bearing mice indicates that chlorella stimulates the natural immune system to protect the body from cancer. Chlorella promotes repair of damaged tissues. It contains up to 10% RNA and 3% DNA. Studies have shown that chlorella helps clear heavy metals, PCB's and other harmful chemicals from the body.

CHLOROPHYLL (Liquid)

Deodorant for the mouth, stomach and intestines. Chlorophyll helps to control intestinal gas. It is useful in intestinal cleansing and in support of acidophilus supplementation. Suggested use is taking one tablespoonful in a glass of water 2 to 4 times daily.

COMFREY LEAF

Demulcent, expectorant, mucilage, vulnerary. Comfrey is a cell proliferator which will help heal broken bones, sprains, and slow-healing sores. It is effective for eliminating bloody urine and for bronchitic conditions. (See Fenu-Comf in Herbal Combination section.)

CRANBERRY

For chronic kidney infections. It is best to take cranberry between meals with at least five glasses of water throughout the day. Seven to nine capsules daily has been shown to be an adequate dosage.
NOTE: Because of the high concentration of sugar in supermarket-type cranberry juice, capsulated powdered cranberries is the preferred way to take this herb.

DAMIANA

Emmenagogue, tonic (especially as a restorative to the reproductive system), sexual stimulant (for females). Damiana helps to balance female hormones.

DANDELION ROOT

Cholagogue, diuretic, hepatic, lithotriptic, stomachic. Dandelion root is an excellent blood purifier for such conditions as dropsy, eczema, and other skin diseases. It is good for enlargement of the liver and for spleen problems. It helps promote the flow of bile in liver disease (especially jaundice, cholecystitis and the primary stages of cirrhosis.) Because of the nutritive salts it contains, dandelion helps build the blood thus eliminating anemia.

DEVIL'S CLAW

Alterative. Devil's claw is a blood cleanser which will remove deposits in the joints and aid in elimination of uric acid from the body. It is used mainly for gout, rheumatism and arthritis.

ECHINACEA

Alterative, antiseptic, lymphatic. Echinacea is one of the best blood purifiers. It is good for blood poisoning, cold and flu prevention, carbuncles, all pus diseases, abscesses of the teeth, gangrene, all lymph swellings, tonsillitis and snake and spider bites. Is often combined with myrrh to rid the body of pus or abscess formation. Echinacea helps build up the supply of large white blood cells. It improves resistance to and recovery from all infections, viral, fungal, as well as bacterial.

EYEBRIGHT

Alterative. Eyebright is valuable in weakness of sight. As a wash, it is used for superficial inflammations of the eye and for conjunctivitis.

FENNEL

Antispasmodic, carminative, galactagogue. Fennel is used for treating gas, acid stomach, colic and cramps. It is sometimes mixed with catnip in tincture form as an aid to colic. (See Catnip & Fennel Extract in Herbal Extracts and Oils section.)

FENUGREEK

Demulcent, emollient, expectorant. Fenugreek is useful for all mucus conditions of the lungs. It helps clean out the bronchial passages of catarrh and other irritants. (See Fenu Comf in Herbal Combinations section.)

FEVERFEW

Prevents attacks of migraines. In one study of 300 users of feverfew, 72% reported that their headaches were less frequent or painful. Feverfew is also shown to be helpful in alleviating inflammation and discomfort of arthritis.

FO-TI

Stimulant, tonic. Fo-ti helps rejuvenate the endocrine glands which, in turn, strengthen the body. Recent scientific studies verify cholesterol-lowering effects of this plant.

GARLIC

Alterative, antibiotic. Garlic is used for all lung and respiratory ailments. It is excellent for both high and low blood pressure, infections, stomach problems and nervous headaches.

Recent laboratory studies have shown that garlic kills viruses. It therefore provides protection against the common cold, amoebic dysentery and other infectious diseases. As an oil, garlic is used for earaches and congested middle ear problems.

Garlic stimulates the production of bile and hydrochloric acid. In other words, garlic is a digestive aid.

GINGER

Carminative, diaphoretic, stimulant. Ginger is used for indigestion, gas, morning sickness and nausea. A study reported in the British medical journal Lancet (March 20, 1982) showed powdered ginger to be more effective than Dramamine against motion sickness. The researchers recommended that a person take two capsules of powdered ginger root 15 minutes before boarding a boat, car or plane. They also stated that ginger has no known toxic effects at normal consumption levels. Ginger root relieves general indigestion, helps dispel gas, eases cramping and relieves spasms of the stomach and colon.

GINKGO

Vasodilator. Ginkgo widens blood vessels, increases circulation and speeds blood flow in the capillaries. It is useful for weakness of hearing and vision, senility and dizziness if the cause is poor circulation. In clinical studies, it was found that patients with inflamed arteries had a reduction of pain. They could walk longer and for greater distances. In 103 patients with ringing in their ears, everyone had a reduction of the ringing. In a group of senile patients, significant improvement was noted after three months of taking ginkgo. It helps with premature memory loss.

CAUTION: People with blood pressure disorders should monitor their blood pressure and consult their doctor about any dramatic changes.

GINSENG, SIBERIAN

Tonic. Siberian ginseng helps the entire body adapt to stress. It brings body systems back into balance and improves stamina in the face of excessive physical and mental exertion.
CAUTION: To be avoided by those who are hyperactive or under high nervous tension.

GOLDEN SEAL HERB

Alterative, antibiotic, antiseptic, emmenagogue, stomachic, tonic. Golden seal is a specific for all problems of the mucus membranes.
CAUTION: Do not use large amounts during pregnancy or if hypoglycemic. When used over a long period of time, golden seal will reduce vitamin B absorption.

GOTU KOLA

Nervine, tonic. Gotu Kola is known in India as a longevity herb. It is used for mental fatigue, poor vitality and senility. It relaxes the nervous system and is considered to be a brain food.

GUAR GUM

Bulking agent. When taken with meals, guar gum aids in a variety of body processes ranging from weight control to the regulation of blood sugar and cholesterol.

Guar gum dissolves in water to form a gel. This allows people on weight loss programs to eat less and still feel full. It appears to slow down both the emptying of the stomach and the intestinal transit time. This would slow down the rate of cholesterol, sugar and fat absorption.

NOTE: To be effective in a weight loss program it is necessary to drink plenty of fluids. A person should start with one capsule three times daily and build up to three capsules three times daily.

HAWTHORN

Circulatory tonic, cardiac. Because it dilates the coronary blood supply and at the same time slows down and stabilizes the contractility of the heart muscle, hawthorn is used for many different heart disturbances. It is excellent for feeble heart action, valvular insufficiency and irregular pulse. It is valuable in angina pectoris or inflammation of the heart muscle.
CAUTION: If symptoms of heart disease are present, see your doctor immediately.

HORSETAIL

Genito-urinary astringent, diuretic, lithotriptic, kidney and bladder tonic. Horsetail is good for kidney disorders, especially kidney stones. It is used for enuresis and other irritable symptoms of the urinary system.
NOTE: Horsetail can be irritating when used for prolonged periods (daily for over a month.) It works best in small, frequent doses (one to two capsules two or three times daily at mealtimes.) People must drink plenty of water when using horsetail.

JUNIPER BERRY

Antispasmodic, diuretic, urinary antiseptic. Juniper berry is used for bladder diseases, intestinal putrefaction, bladder and ureteral infections (cystitis), gout and for other arthritic conditions associated with acid waste.
CAUTION: Not intended for use when kidneys are inflamed or during pregnancy.

KAVA KAVA

Anodyne, antiseptic, antispasmodic, diuretic. Kava kava is an excellent herb for insomnia and nervousness. It will invoke sleep and relax the nervous system. CAUTION: To be taken in small dosages for short periods of time. Long term usage of high dosages can interfere with elimination of toxins from the liver.

KELP

Demulcent, nutritive, thyroid restorative. Kelp is used for thyroid diseases of any description. It is rich in iodine which the thyroid needs to function. Kelp stimulates metabolism and is therefore most helpful in the nourishment of the body. Studies at McGill University found a factor in kelp called sodium alginate. This binds radioactive strontium 90 in the intestines and carries it out of the body.

LICORICE

Demulcent, expectorant, laxative, restorative and stimulant to the adrenal glands. Licorice induces the adrenal cortex to produce cortisone and aldosterone. It is one of the best-known herbs for hypoglycemia. CAUTION: Large doses of licorice root should be avoided by people with high blood pressure or those using digitalis drugs. Potassium supplementation is encouraged while using licorice.

MARSHMALLOW

Demulcent, diuretic, emollient, lithotriptic. Marshmallow root is one third mucilage and therefore one of the best remedies to lubricate the kidneys, intestines and lungs in cases of infection and inflammation. It is used in combination with other diuretic herbs during kidney treatment to assist in the release of stones and gravel. Using two to six grams of dried root three or four times daily helps soothe inflamed urinary passages, hiatus hernia, peptic ulceration and other internal inflammation.

MILK THISTLE

Cholagogue, liver tonic. Milk thistle regenerates liver cells and protects them against the action of liver poison. It aids the rehabilitation process after acute hepatitis, gall-bladder disease or exposure to alcohol, drug or chemical pollution abuse. The seed extract is used and may be sold under the name "Thisilyn" or "Silymarin." (For more information on milk thistle, see "Liver" in the Herbal Combinations section.)

MYRRH GUM

Antiseptic, emmenagogue. Because it is such a powerful antiseptic, myrrh is often used in equal parts with golden seal for intestinal ulcers, bad breath, catarrh of the intestines, and all other mucus membrane conditions. CAUTION: Myrrh gum should not be taken in large amounts or over a long period of time.

NETTLE

Alterative, astringent, nutritive. Nettle is traditionally used to help relieve the discomfort and problems associated with asthma. It is used for any type of internal hemorrhage. Because it stimulates production of hydrochloric acid and bile, it helps in the digestive process.

OAT FIBER

Oat fiber is more effective than ANY other medication for reducing cholesterol. A person should take one capsule three times daily and work up to three capsules three times daily.

PARSLEY

Strong diuretic. Parsley is used in cases of difficult urination, dropsy and kidney stones. Combined with echinacea, plantain and marshmallow root, it is a good remedy for kidney and bladder infection. Parsley is used for arthritic conditions linked to defective kidney eliminations.
CAUTION: Parsley can be warming and should not be used if the kidney is inflamed. Avoid heavy consumption of this herb during pregnancy.

PSYLLIUM

Demulcent, laxative. Psyllium assists in easy evacuation by increasing water in the colon. It will thereby make bowel movements easier for people with colitis and hemorrhoids. A teaspoon of the powder in warm water or juice three times a day will clean the intestine, removing putrefactive toxins. For children, the dose is one half a teaspoon. Fluid intake should be increased when taking psyllium.

Psyllium is sold under the trade name "Fibresyl."

CAUTION: Psyllium or other bulking agents should be avoided in cases of bowel obstructions or perforations. Because psyllium forms an indigestible mass, it should be taken at times different than other supplements.

RED CLOVER

Alterative. Red Clover is an excellent blood purifier when used alone or in combination with yellow dock, dandelion root, sassafras or other blood purifiers. It is especially useful in chronic skin conditions such as psoriasis or eczema. Long-term usage may be required to achieve optimal results.

RED RASPBERRY

Antispasmodic, astringent, tonic (for the uterus and mucus membranes.) Red raspberry is used for relief of urinary irritation and for soothing the kidneys and the whole urinary tract. Strengthening the walls of the uterus, it is often used during pregnancy as an aid to ease in childbirth and in alleviating morning sickness.

Two red raspberry capsules three times daily is a highly effective remedy for chronic diarrhea.

Red raspberry may be used in capsule or tea form. (For tea, steep 2-8 grams of dried leaf and drink three times per day.)

SARSAPARILLA

Alterative, carminative, tonic, testosterone precursor. Sarsaparilla assists in the elimination of urea and uric acid and is thus used for skin eruptions, arthritis and gout. It is also a tonic to the endocrine system.

Sarsaparilla is widely used by athletes as a natural alternative to steroids and as a source of precursors of muscle-building hormones. That is to say, sarsaparilla will help a person increase his muscle bulk IF he is working out. A good dosage for someone working hard in a gym is two capsules three times daily.

SCULLCAP

Antispasmodic, nervine, central nervous system relaxant and restorative. Scullcap is an excellent nervine for almost any nervous system malfunction. It has been used as an aid in weaning people from excessive use of Valium and barbiturates. Scullcap is soothing to the nerves, relaxing and sleep inducing. It is used for neurological and neuromotor conditions, including epilepsy, helping to reduce the severity and frequency of symptoms.

SENNA

Laxative, vermifuge. This effective laxative should be combined with ginger or fennel to prevent cramping. It will help to eliminate most types of worms from the colon if used following wormwood. CAUTION: Senna should not be used in cases of piles, prolapsed intestine or inflammation anywhere in the intestinal tract. DO NOT USE DURING PREGNANCY.

SLIPPERY ELM

Anti-diarrheal (especially for children,) demulcent, emollient, nutritive. In cases of dysentery and other digestive upsets, slippery elm is an excellent herb to settle the spasmodic reaction of the colon and bowels.

SUMA

Adaptogen, tonic. Suma is an ideal tonic for women who desire natural hormone balance without the use of traditionally "male" tonics like Korean ginseng. Suma will produce estrogen (see glossary) if the body needs it; it will not produce more estrogen than the body can handle. It is the richest known source of naturally-occurring germanium. Germanium is believed to enhance the flow of oxygen to the cells.

WHITE WILLOW

Anodyne, antispasmodic, tonic. White willow was used to make the first aspirin. It alleviates pain and reduces fever.

UVA URSI

Astringent, diuretic. Uva ursi is a specific for nephritis, cystitis, urethritis and kidney and bladder stones. When used for those purposes, it should be combined with another diuretic such as marshmallow root.

CAUTION: Uva Ursi is a vasoconstrictor to the uterus (cuts down blood flow to the uterus.) It should therefore not be used in large quantities during pregnancy.

VALERIAN

Antispasmodic, nervine. Valerian is a strong sedative and one of the best nerve tonics. It is an excellent remedy for people under emotional stress or pain.

WHITE OAK

Astringent. White oak is helpful for ulcerated bladders and bloody urine. It is taken for hemorrhage of the intestines, lungs, bowels and kidneys.

YELLOW DOCK

Alterative, astringent, laxative, cholagogue. Yellow dock tones up the entire body and is used for such conditions as skin infections, tumors, liver and gall bladder problems and ulcers. It stimulates the flow of bile, and is therefore slightly laxative. Being high in iron, it is used in the treatment of anemia and in skin problems, especially where the cause is associated with constipation or liver disfunction.

YUCCA

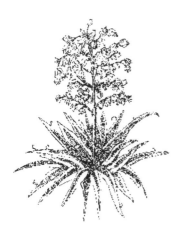

Alterative. This herb is one of nature's best blood purifiers. It is especially good for arthritis and rheumatism.

HERBAL COMBINATIONS

Herbal combinations consist of two or more herbs, carefully selected and compounded to feed a specific area of the body. A single herb often does not have all of the therapeutic qualities that are needed. The combinations in this book are presented for the express purpose of making it easy for the layman to use herbal combinations.

The quantities shown under "Suggested Use" are for adults weighing approximately 150 pounds. Decrease use when using herbal remedies for children or the elderly.

To ensure that the herbs in a capsule are assimilated, they should always be taken with a full glass of water or else made into a tea by emptying the contents of a capsule into a cup of boiling water and steeping for 3 to 5 minutes.

ADRENAL GLANDS

HERBS: AdrenAid/AD-R - Mullein leaves, licorice root, gotu kola herb, cayenne, ginger root, Siberian ginseng bark and hawthorn berries.

PHYSIOLOGIC ACTION: This combination helps maintain a healthy adrenal gland. It is especially useful when the body has been subjected to excess stress including coffee and other stimulant products. Stress can weaken and overburden normal adrenal function.

SUGGESTED USE: Two or three capsules three times daily one-half hour before meals.

ALLERGIES

HERBS: HAS - Chaparral, lobelia, parsley, Brigham Tea, marshmallow root, burdock root, cayenne and golden seal.

PHYSIOLOGIC ACTION: HAS relaxes bronchial spasms, opens bronchial tubes and eases breathing for the temporary relief of bronchial asthma and hay fever. Although it works best if taken daily during allergy season, HAS can also be taken in response to individual attacks. HAS contains a natural antihistamine and helps decongest the sinus and other mucus-holding tissues.

SUGGESTED USE: Take two capsules three times daily. Best results can be expected when this formula is used in conjunction with a low-mucus diet. (See index.)

ANTI-BACTERIAL

HERB: Garlicin (odor-controlled garlic)

PHYSIOLOGIC ACTION: Garlicin contains the active principles of fresh garlic that are known to kill bacteria, viruses associated with the common cold and fungi. It also helps to reduce high blood pressure. In independent tests comparing Garlicin with other odor-controlled garlics and with fresh garlic, Garlicin was closest to fresh garlic in its ability to kill Candida albicans (yeast.) In this test, Garlicin was more than twice as potent as its nearest competitor.

Garlicin has also shown activity in preventing blood platelet aggregation. Thus it can play an effective role as part of an overall dietary program to help prevent strokes, heart attacks and internal blood clotting.

Because it stimulates the production of bile and hydrochloric acid, Garlicin can also be considered a digestive aid.

SUGGESTED USE: Take one capsule one or two times daily with water. For special dietary programs, build gradually up to two capsules three times daily.

NOTE: Take just before a meal to prevent garlic breath. After three years of testing, the manufacturer discovered that it was impossible to take all of the odor-causing agents out of garlic and still have a product that was practically as effective as the real thing. CAUTION: Garlic should not be taken by hemophiliacs.

ARTHRITIS AND RHEUMATISM

HERBS: RHEUM-AID/YUCCA-AR - Yucca, hydrangea, Brigham tea, burdock root, chaparral, black walnut leaves, wild lettuce, sarsaparilla root, wormwood, valerian root, lobelia, cayenne, black cohosh root.

PHYSIOLOGIC ACTION: This special formula helps relieve symptoms associated with: bursitis, calcification, gout, rheumatoid arthritis, rheumatism, and osteoarthritis. It helps the body reduce or eliminate swelling and inflammation in the body's joints and connective tissue and helps to relieve stiffness and pain. Gout patients have had excellent results by combining burdock root capsules with Yucca-AR.

For further information on arthritis, see Diet section and also the index.

SUGGESTED USE: Begin with the equivalent of one capsule twice daily with a glass of water. Gradually increase the amount over the next two or three weeks to the equivalent of two capsules three times daily. Then regulate as desired.

BLOOD CLEANSER

HERBS: CS - Gentian, heal all, catnip, golden seal root, bayberry bark, myrrh gum, Irish moss, fenugreek seed, comfrey root, bugleweed, yellow dock root, blue vervain, prickly ash bark, violet leaves, Brigham tea, red clover blossoms, cascara sagrada bark, chickweed and cyani flowers.

PHYSIOLOGIC ACTION: Clean blood is a key to recovering and sustaining health. Body toxins, mucus and other wastes are more easily removed with this herbal aid. CS is effective as a total body system cleanser.

SUGGESTED USE: Take one capsule per day in the first week, building to two capsules three times daily over a six week period.

BLOOD PRESSURE (High)

HERBS: CAYENNE-GARLIC - Cayenne and garlic

PHYSIOLOGIC ACTION: Cayenne-Garlic plays an important role in an overall dietary and exercise program to help in lowering the blood pressure. It helps to relieve colds, influenza, and general infections; it strengthens the heart and improves blood circulation.

SUGGESTED USE: Take one to four capsules two to three times daily as part of an overall dietary and exercise program to improve circulation and general health.

BLOOD PRESSURE (High or Low)

HERBS: B/P - Cayenne, parsley, ginger root, golden seal root, garlic and Siberian ginseng.

PHYSIOLOGIC ACTION: With a unique combination of well known herbs, this formulation improves overall blood circulation and tends to adjust high or low pressure to the body's normal level. Cholesterol build-up in the blood vessels can also be reduced.

SUGGESTED USE: Take 2 to 4 capsules 3 times daily.

BLOOD PURIFIER - GENERAL DETOXIFIER

HERBS: RED CLOVER COMBINATION - Red clover blossoms, chaparral, licorice root, peach bark, Oregon grape root, echinacea, cascara sagrada bark, sarsaparilla root, prickly ash bark, burdock root and buckthorn bark.

PHYSIOLOGIC ACTION: Nearly identical to the famous Hoxey formula, this formula effectively aids the body's cleansing systems, especially the bloodstream. It should be included as a nutritional supplement in all treatment of chronic or degenerative conditions and can be used with any detoxification program.

SUGGESTED USE: Take two capsules daily, increasing to three capsules three times daily.

BONE, FLESH AND CARTILAGE BUILDER

HERBS: B F&C - White oak bark, comfrey herb, marshmallow, mullein, black walnut hulls, gravel root and scullcap.

PHYSIOLOGIC ACTION: B F&C is designed to aid the healing processes involved with broken bones, athletic injuries, sprained limbs, and related inflammation and swelling. B F&C is a tonic that can be used after acute and chronic diseases to help rebuild the body. It is effective as a skin wash for itchy, irritated skin in children and adults. B F&C also may be used in tea form: one teaspoon to one cup of boiling water; steep for 20 minutes.

It is possible to buy B F&C in ointment form. B F&C Ointment relieves pain and blistering of sunburn and is effective against frostbite. It helps to heal cuts, abrasions and open sores. The ointment can be soothing to muscle aches and pains. It is effective against diaper rash, minor burns, bruises and torn ligaments.

SUGGESTED USE: (1)The equivalent of two capsules three times a day, or (2)Apply directly as a fomentation by covering affected area with a cloth soaked with strong Bone, Flesh and Cartilage tea or B F&C Ointment. Wrap with plastic to protect clothes and bedding during the night. Continue until relief is obtained. In ointment or fomentation form, B F&C will actually feed the body through the pores.

BREATHING DIFFICULTIES - See Respiratory

BOWEL FUNCTIONS - See Lower Bowel and Laxatives

CALCIUM DEFICIENCY (CRAMPS, NERVES, TEETH)

HERBS: Ca-T - Horsetail grass, comfrey herb, oat straw and scullcap.

PHYSIOLOGIC ACTION: Organic calcium, silica, and other tranquillizing minerals in this formula help prevent cramps ("Charlie horses"). This is a natural way to calm nerves and aid sleep in addition to rebuilding the nerve sheath, vein and artery walls, teeth and bones.

SUGGESTED USE: Take two capsules three times daily.

For a teething child: a fever may be present. This is because Nature is attempting to draw calcium from the body to feed the teeth. Bring Ca-T (1 tsp./cup of water) to a boil. Simmer down to one half volume. Add fruit juice or raw sugar to make more palatable. Refrigerate. When child starts fussing, feed him/her a teaspoonful of the warmed liquid. Expect a tooth to have emerged within the next 24 hours.

CAUTION: Not intended for use during pregnancy.

An alternative calcium supplement is:

FEM-CAL - Calcium carbonate, calcium citrate, magnesium, copper, manganese and boron.

PHYSIOLOGIC ACTION: Fem-Cal combines the high potency of calcium carbonate with the high bioavailability of calcium citrate. It has 25% of the U.S. RDA of calcium.

SUGGESTED USE: One tablet 1 to 4 times daily at mealtimes and/or bedtime.

COLDS AND COUGHS

HERBS: Fenu-Comf - Fenugreek seed and comfrey leaves.

PHYSIOLOGIC ACTION: Both fenugreek seeds and comfrey have been used effectively in relieving cold symptoms, helping to dissolve mucus and restore free breathing. This formula is also helpful in relieving asthma, bronchitis, hay fever, and mucus in the lungs.

SUGGESTED USE: Two or three capsules every three hours with water.

COLDS AND FLU

HERBS: C&F - Garlic, rose hips, parsley, watercress and rosemary.

PHYSIOLOGIC ACTION: C&F helps the body in cases of influenza or colds. In addition, C&F supplies vitamins, minerals and other factors that help prevent viral infections. It will help relieve fevers and a runny nose.

SUGGESTED USE: Take two capsules every two to four hours.

COLD PREVENTION

HERBS: HERBAL COMPOSITION - Bayberry bark, ginger root, cloves, cayenne and white pine bark.

PHYSIOLOGIC ACTION: Take prior to winter season or when first signs of the flu, chills, fever, etc. appear. Herbal Composition will help relieve symptoms of colds and flu, viral infections, cold extremities, and will promote circulation. Herbal Composition can also help settle an upset stomach.

SUGGESTED USE: Two capsules every hour with a glass of warm water or catnip tea until perspiration flows freely. When perspiration stops, repeat process. During cold and flu season, take three to four capsules hourly if necessary.

DIGESTION

HERBS: Primadophilus - Lactobacillus acidophilus and L. casei subspecies rhamnosus.

PHYSIOLOGIC ACTION: Primadophilus is a milk-free, high potency, enteric coated acidophilus. It helps maintain healthy intestinal activity, improves digestion and elimination and increases the ratio of "friendly" bacteria in the intestines. The unique culture of Primadophilus is effective against 25 different harmful bacteria, including salmonella, staph and strep.

When putrefying bacteria colonize in large numbers in the throat, tongue and mouth, a coated tongue can result causing halitosis (bad breath.) When these same types of bacteria grow unchecked in the intestines, they produce objectionable gases. Supplementation with Primadophilus is a good way to maintain a healthy intestinal floral balance and keep putrefactive bacteria under control.

Antibiotics kill off "friendly" as well as harmful bacteria in the intestines. This can lead to incomplete digestion of food, diarrhea and even yeast infection. It is therefore wise to take Primadophilus during and after treatment with an antibiotic drug. Cold sores are caused by a virus (Herpes simplex Type 1) that can be reduced or eliminated with Primadophilus.

SUGGESTED USE: One capsule per day after a meal. For an intensive treatment, usage can be increased to three caps per day after two weeks.

Other digestive aids are **COMFREY PEPSIN** and **COMFREY PLUS**. These two formulas are for occasional use only. Suggested use in both cases is 2 capsules, 3 times daily at mealtimes.

DIURETIC

HERBS: KB-2 - Buchu leaves, pellitory-of-the-wall, uva ursi leaves extract, couchgrass root, marshmallow root.

PHYSIOLOGIC ACTION: Increases the flow of urine.

SUGGESTED USE: For the occasional relief of water retention take 2 capsules 2 or 3 times daily.

(Where KB-2 is not available, **KB** may be substituted.)

EYE DISORDERS

HERBS: HERBAL EYEBRIGHT FORMULA - Eyebright, golden seal root, bayberry bark, red raspberry leaves and cayenne.

PHYSIOLOGIC ACTION: This herbal formula is extremely valuable in strengthening and healing the eyes. It can aid the body in dissolving cataracts and healing lesions and eye injuries.

SUGGESTED USE: Take 2 capsules 3 times daily with water. Best results will be obtained when following a low-mucus diet. (See index.) Use of this product during or following a cleansing program is also helpful.

FATIGUE, STRESS AND CHRONIC ILLNESS

HERBS: HERBAL UP/GINSENG GOTU KOLA PLUS
Siberian Ginseng, Gotu Kola, Bee Pollen and Cayenne.

PHYSIOLOGIC ACTION: This formula is therapeutic for many symptoms: it builds energy and stamina, increases mental and physical powers, combats stress and weariness, improves reflexes, helps the body to defend itself against various toxins, normalizes low blood pressure and mild cases of high blood pressure, benefits nerve systems and functions and promotes cell rebuilding.

SUGGESTED USE: Take two capsules three times daily.

An alternative energy formula is the

ENERGIZER FORMULA - 200 i.u. Vitamin E, Korean White ginseng, bee pollen, lecithin and wheat germ oil.

PHYSIOLOGIC ACTION: As a "pick-me-up" to restore energy or relieve simple fatigue.

SUGGESTED USE: One or two capsules daily at mealtimes.

A third energy alternative is: **CoQ10** - A necessary nutrient for production of energy at the cellular level.

PHYSIOLOGIC ACTION: CoQ10 allows the mitochondria (energy producers in each cell -- see glossary) to efficiently convert our food into energy. A deficiency of CoQ10 in our cells can be compared to a car engine badly out of tune. Even though there is plenty of fuel available, the engine cannot convert it into energy efficiently. Because the mitochondria produce 95% of the body's energy, a deficiency of CoQ10 will affect the performance of all organs and systems.

Studies show that the CoQ10 level decreases with age. Dietary supplementation with CoQ10 can offset deficiencies of this nutrient caused by aging, will improve energy utilization and keep the body's functions running "in tune."

FEVER/FLU COMPLAINTS

HERBS: FENU-THYME - Fenugreek seed and thyme.

PHYSIOLOGIC ACTION: This is a formula designed to alleviate flu discomfort. It helps reduce fever and mucus build-up in the body. Thyme has anti-bacterial and anti-viral activity.

SUGGESTED USE: Take two capsules two to five times daily.

GLAND PROBLEMS

HERBS: GL - Mullein, calendula and scullcap.

PHYSIOLOGIC ACTION: GL is helpful for swollen glands and lymph nodes and in helping the body fight infections. Since this may be a sign of more serious infections, if swelling does not reduce within two weeks, consult a qualified health professional.

SUGGESTED USE: Take two capsules two times daily.

GLANDULAR INFECTIONS including EAR INFECTIONS

HERBS: IGL - Echinacea, barberry root bark, and ginger.

PHYSIOLOGIC ACTION: Especially effective for healing the lymphatic system, this combination is a natural aid in fighting mumps or infections in the glands, ears, breasts, throat and lungs.

SUGGESTED USE: Take 2 capsules 2 to 3 times daily.

HEADACHES

HERBS: FUSHO ESSENTIAL OIL - Menthol, camphor and eucalyptus.

PHYSIOLOGIC ACTION: The heat from Fusho Oil penetrates the temple and neck to relieve pressure which can cause headaches. (For more information on headaches, see "feverfew" in the single herbs section.)

SUGGESTED USE: HEADACHES: Rub a drop onto each temple and the back of the neck.
SORE THROAT: Place a drop onto finger. Transfer this into back of throat.
UPSET STOMACH: Drink a drop of FuSho in a half cup of water.
SORE MUSCLES: Massage FuSho into muscles.
MOSQUITO BITES: One drop on a mosquito bite relieves itch quickly.

HEART

HERBS: H-Hawthorn, cayenne, vitamin E and lecithin.

PHYSIOLOGIC ACTION: The "H" combination promotes elasticity of arteries. This remarkable formula not only helps reduce cholesterol but also aids in rebuilding the heart muscle, strengthening and regulating the heartbeat and improving circulation in general.

SUGGESTED USE: Take 4 capsules daily, 2 in the morning and 2 at night. If heart problems exist, see your doctor.

HORMONE IMBALANCE: See MENOPAUSE and IMPOTENCE

HYPOGLYCEMIA

HERBS: HIGL-Licorice root, cedar berries, juniper berries, wild yam and dandclion root.

PHYSIOLOGIC ACTION: HIGL acts to correct glandular malfunctions and the subsequent imbalance in hypoglycemia. It feeds and stimulates the adrenal glands and pancreas so that blood sugar levels can return to normal. By restoring the adrenals, this formula is an aid to handling stress.

SUGGESTED USE: Take 2 capsules 3 times daily with water. Dietary changes are also necessary for hypoglycemia. Consult a health care professional.

IMMUNE SUPPORT

HERBS: IM-AID - Echinacea root, thyme herbs, hyssop, chaparral, hawthorn berries, Irish moss, mullein leaves, Korean white ginseng, rosemary.

PHYSIOLOGIC ACTION: IM-AID is designed to help fight infections and stimulate the immune response. This formula is especially helpful in rebuilding the body during convalescence and as a preventative during colds and flu season.

SUGGESTED USE: Take 2 capsules 3 times daily with water at mealtimes. Dose can be increased gradually during cold and flu season.

IMPOTENCE

HERBS: APH - Damiana, Siberian ginseng, echinacea, fo-ti, gotu kola, sarsaparilla root and saw palmetto.

PHYSIOLOGIC ACTION: APH has natural precursors to testosterone. As such it is used both as a substitute for steroids (see sarsaparilla) and as an aid in handling impotence. APH is formulated to restore normal hormone balance and stimulate male and female sexual impulses as well as strengthens and increases sexual power. It is also effective in helping to eliminate fatigue.

SUGGESTED USE: Take two capsules three times daily.

INFECTIONS

HERBS: IF - Plantain, black walnut leaves, calendula, golden seal root, marshmallow root, bugleweed.

PHYSIOLOGIC ACTION: Helpful in cleansing swollen lymph nodes and fighting infections throughout the body.

SUGGESTED USE: Take 2 capsules 3 or 4 times daily.

INSOMNIA

HERBS: SILENT NIGHT/E-Z-SLEEP - Hops flowers, valerian root and scullcap.

PHYSIOLOGIC ACTION: This is a combination of herbs that soothes stress and promotes a peaceful and natural sleep. It is used as an herbal relaxant.

SUGGESTED USE: Take two to six capsules prior to bedtime. For best results in cases of prolonged insomnia, take two capsules of this formula or 3 Ex-Stress/Calm-Aid 4 to 6 hours before bedtime and 2 to 6 capsules at bedtime.

KIDNEY FUNCTIONS

HERBS: GARLIC and PARSLEY - Garlic and parsley

PHYSIOLOGIC ACTION: This combination is known to promote urine flow and strengthen the kidneys. Garlic and Parsley also helps revitalize and strengthen the liver and spleen.

SUGGESTED USE: Take two capsules three times daily.

LAXATIVES

HERBS: NATURALAX/MULTILAX #1 - Psyllium husks, senna leaves

PHYSIOLOGIC ACTION: Helps relieve minor constipation.

SUGGESTED USE: Two capsules each evening before retiring.

CAUTION: Do not use when abdominal pain, nausea or vomiting are present. Frequent or prolonged use of any laxative may result in dependence. Keep out of the reach of children.
Another laxative formula is:

ALOELAX - This is a very strong laxative only for those with chronic or severe constipation. It usually provides relief within 12 to 18 hours. Aloelax is not recommended for the elderly or for pregnant women.

A third laxative is **NATURALAX/MULTILAX #3**. This combination is not quite as strong as Aloelax. It is recommended for those who require strong, rapid relief within 6 to 8 hours.

CAUTION: Intestinal cleansers should not be used when people suffer from abdominal pain, nausea or vomiting.

LIVER

HERBS: THISILYN - Milk thistle seed extract (contains 80% silymarin)

PHYSIOLOGIC ACTION: A specialized extract, Thisilyn helps to protect the liver and neutralize some poisons. Its antioxidant quality helps prevent free radical damage in the liver.

In human studies, silymarin had significant positive effects in treating liver diseases including cirrhosis and chronic hepatitis. Among other things, silymarin stimulates the production of new liver cells. Because it improves liver function, silymarin has been of great benefit to patients with psoriasis. It helps rebuild the liver after steroid or alcohol abuse.

A number of poison control centers in West Germany use extract of milk thistle.

SUGGESTED USE: Take one capsule two or three times daily with water before mealtime.

LIVER and GALL BLADDER

HERBS: LIVERON/LG - Barberry root bark, wild yam, cramp bark, fennel seed, ginger root, catnip and peppermint.

PHYSIOLOGIC ACTION: This formula acts as an aid to the cleansing of the liver and gall bladder. Both of theses glands are subsequently strengthened and function is improved. This formula can also be used to relieve intestinal gas. Because LG helps improve sluggish bile production, it helps in cases of poor fat and fatty acid digestion.

SUGGESTED USE: Take two capsules three times daily.

LOWER BOWEL CLEANSER, TONIC

HERBS: NATURALAX/MULTILAX #2-Cascara sagrada bark, barberry root bark, ginger root, golden seal root, lobelia, red raspberry leaves, Turkey rhubarb root, fennel seed and cayenne.

PHYSIOLOGIC ACTION: This combination of toning herbs naturally accelerates internal cleansing of the body through the bowels. It helps loosen and eliminate old, toxic fecal matter and encrustations including mucus buildup, thereby increasing food and water assimilation. It feeds the peristaltic muscles of the system. It is best to use this formula until the bowel is clean, healed, and performing normally.

SUGGESTED USE: Take two capsules three times daily.

CAUTION: Do not take during pregnancy. As with all laxatives, keep out of reach of children.

MEMORY AID

HERBS: REMEM/SEN - Blue vervain, blessed thistle, gotu kola, ginger root, cayenne, Brigham tea.

PHYSIOLOGIC ACTION:

The herbs in this formula help to nourish the brain cells and tissues and improve their ability to perform mental functions.

SUGGESTED USE: Take two capsules two times daily.

An alternate memory aid is GINKGOLD. (See single herb section.)

MENSTRUATION

HERBS: FEM-MEND/FC - Golden seal root, blessed thistle, cayenne, uva ursi leaves, cramp bark, false unicorn root, red raspberry leaves, squaw vine, and ginger root.

PHYSIOLOGIC ACTION: This combination helps regulate the female menstrual cycle. It relieve cramps, flooding and pain.
CAUTION: Do not take Fem-Mend/FC while taking estrogen or oral contraceptives, as it may interfere with the actions of synthetic hormones.

SUGGESTED USE: Take 1 or 2 capsules 2 to 3 times daily.

MENOPAUSE

HERBS: CHANGE-O-LIFE/MP - Black cohosh, sarsaparilla root, Siberian ginseng, licorice root, false unicorn root, blessed thistle and squaw vine.

PHYSIOLOGIC ACTION: This unique formula aids in the function and development of hormone balance in both males and females. MP is good during menopause for relief of hot flashes and accompanying headaches, nervousness and menstrual discharge.

SUGGESTED USE: Take 1 or 2 capsules, 2 or 3 times daily with meals. During extreme difficulties one can take 3 capsules, 3 times daily for up to one month.

CAUTION: Not for use during pregnancy.

MOTION SICKNESS

HERBS: MOTION MATE - Ginger root, meadow sweet herb, peppermint leaves, red raspberry leaves and hyssop.

PHYSIOLOGIC ACTION: This combination is used to prevent and/or relieve simple symptoms of travel or motion sickness.

SUGGESTED USE: Take three capsules with water 30 minutes before boarding a plane, car or boat. If nausea still occurs, take 3 to 7 capsules per hour while travelling. (Also see "ginger" in the single herbs section.)

NERVOUS DISORDERS

HERBS: EX-STRESS/CALM-AID - Black cohosh root, cayenne, hops, scullcap, wood betony, valerian root, lady's slipper.

PHYSIOLOGIC ACTION: This is an excellent formula for soothing and restoring the whole nervous system, to relieve nervous tension and rebuild the nerve sheaths. This is also an excellent aid for insomnia, and stress-related conditions. It helps overcome effects of overwork and fatigue.

SUGGESTED USE: Take one or two capsules two or three times daily.

PAIN, HEADACHES, NERVOUS TENSION

HERBS: A-P - Wild lettuce, valerian root and cayenne.

PHYSIOLOGIC ACTION: This combination is used to relieve pain in any part of the body. AP is a natural way to ease chronic pain, headaches, childbirth after-pains, aching teeth, nervous tension, spasms, intestinal gas and whooping cough.

SUGGESTED USE: Take two to six capsules as needed.

PANCREAS

HERBS: PC - Cedar berries, uva ursi leaves, licorice root, mullein, cayenne and golden seal root.

PHYSIOLOGIC ACTION: To help arrest infection and remove sedimentation and mucus, PC contains natural hormones within the formula that help the pancreas restore itself. This combination is also used for blood-sugar problems and for healing the spleen.

A significant number of people with maturity onset diabetes have reduced or eliminated their insulin requirements by using PC and making appropriate dietary changes.

CAUTION: Do not discontinue use of insulin without consulting your doctor.

SUGGESTED USE: Take two capsules three times daily.

PARASITES

HERBS: PK - Absinthe, male fern, tansy leaves, black walnut hulls, comfrey leaves, mullein leaves, fennel seed, and cascara sagrada bark.

PHYSIOLOGIC ACTION: PK is useful in destroying and eliminating internal parasites such as worms.
SUGGESTED USE: Take 1 to 3 capsules, 3 times daily for 1 month. Discontinue for 1 month and then resume.

CAUTION: Do not take if pregnant.

PROLAPSUS

HERBS: YELLOW DOCK FORMULA - White oak bark, comfrey leaves, yellow dock root, mullein, black walnut leaves, marshmallow root and calendula.

PHYSIOLOGIC ACTION: This formula can be used to help revitalize a prolapsed uterus. It is also effective in helping alleviate hemorrhoids, colitis, and in cleansing and purifying programs.

SUGGESTED USE: Take two capsules three times daily.

PROSTATE AND KIDNEY

HERBS: PR - Cayenne, uva ursi leaves, parsley, golden seal root, gravel root, juniper berries, marshmallow root, ginger root and Siberian ginseng.

PHYSIOLOGIC ACTION: PR is useful in aiding the body to arrest infection, sedimentation, or inflammation of the prostate and to dissolve kidney stones.

SUGGESTED USE: Take two capsules twice daily.

RESPIRATORY

HERBS: Breathe-Aid/BRE - Marshmallow root, mullein, comfrey leaves, lobelia, chickweed and euphorbia.

PHYSIOLOGIC ACTION: This natural herbal formula effectively relieves irritation and promotes healing throughout the entire respiratory tract.

SUGGESTED USE: Take 2 capsules 3 times daily, preferably at mealtime. Best results can be expected when this formula is used in conjunction with a low-mucus diet. (See index.)

SKIN BLEMISHES

HERBS: AKN - Dandelion root, sarsaparilla root, burdock root, licorice root, echinacea, yellow dock root, kelp, cayenne, and chaparral.

PHYSIOLOGIC ACTION: When toxins are eliminated from the body via the skin, this important herbal formula helps cleanse the bloodstream. "Pimples," blackheads, and other superficial skin eruptions, and more serious conditions such as boils, carbuncles, dermatitis, eczema, and pruritus will be more effectively eliminated when the blood has been cleansed.

SUGGESTED USE: Take two capsules three times daily. Also increase intake of water or fluids to 6-8 glasses daily.

SKIN

HERBS: HERBAL MINERAL/MK-9 - Alfalfa leaves, kelp, chickweed, parsley and dandelion root.

PHYSIOLOGIC ACTION: An excellent source of natural vitamins and minerals, this formula promotes healing and prevents itching, scaling, and inflammation of the skin. It is also a nutritional aid in stubborn cases of acne.

Herbal Mineral contains naturally chelated TRACE MINERALS. (Some of the most critical minerals are trace minerals and may not be included in your present diet.)

SUGGESTED USE: Take two capsules three times daily.

See also: Single herbs, ointments and tinctures.

STOMACH

See **DIGESTION** and also **TINCTURES**

THYROID

HERBS: T - Mullein, parsley, kelp, Irish moss, Iceland moss, black walnut and passion flower.

PHYSIOLOGIC ACTION: To balance metabolism, this formula revitalizes and promotes healing of the thyroid. Thereby, it can help relieve nervous tension which may be caused or aggravated by a weak or improperly functioning thyroid.

SUGGESTED USE: Two capsules two times daily. Additional kelp may prove helpful. (See single herb section.)

ULCERS

HERBS: MYRRH-GOLDEN SEAL PLUS - Myrrh gum, golden seal root and cayenne.

PHYSIOLOGIC ACTION: This combination provides ingredients needed by the body to heal ulcers, cuts, wounds, bruises, sprains and burns. It is good as a poultice for external wounds and is also helpful when used as a gargle.

SUGGESTED USE: Take two capsules daily.

WEIGHT CONTROL

HERBS: HERBAL SLIM/SKC - Chickweed, safflower, burdock root, parsley, kelp, licorice root, fennel seed, echinacea, black walnut hulls, papaya leaves and hawthorn berries.

PHYSIOLOGIC ACTION: SKC is very effective in cleansing the bowels and eliminating excess water. At the same time it appeases the appetite and helps to dissolve excess fat.

This formula reduces tension often associated with dieting.

SUGGESTED USE: As a dietary supplement, use the equivalent of two capsules 30 minutes before mealtime with a glass of water. As with all weight control programs, SKC is to be used in conjunction with a diet and exercise program.

YEAST (CANDIDA ALBICANS)

HERB: Caprinex (sodium caprylate)

PHYSIOLOGIC ACTION: Combats yeast and fungus problems.

NOTE: Candida albicans is normally found in the human body and is harmless when kept under control. However, a person's dietary choices can cause an imbalance and therefore a yeast infection. For instance, the antibiotics in commercial meats can destroy "friendly" bacteria in our intestines. Suddenly the bacteria-fungi ratio is out of balance and the candida albicans can multiply rapidly. This natural formula can help the body regain control over candida.

A Caprinex program to combat yeast is more effective when combined with a Primadophilus program.

SUGGESTED USE: Over a two week period gradually build up to 2 or 3 capsules 3 times daily with water at mealtimes. In severe cases of candida the die-off rate and subsequent release of toxins is often too great for many to withstand. A gradual program might prove better. Maintenance dosage: 1 capsule 3 times daily.

HERBAL EXTRACTS, OILS and OINTMENTS

ANTIBIOTIC OIL

HERBS: OIL OF GARLIC - Olive oil and fresh garlic.

PHYSIOLOGIC ACTION: This product can be used internally or externally for infections, earaches, sore throats, stiffness in the joints, moles, warts, etc. The beneficial properties of garlic are well established.

SUGGESTED USE: Apply externally, pat or rub into affected area, or add three to six drops to cup of hot water.

ANTI-MUCUS TINCTURE

HERBS: ELDERBERRY EXTRACT: Distilled water, elderberry, alcohol and vegetable glycerine.

PHYSIOLOGIC ACTION: High in potassium, elderberry may improve the body's performance in discharging and reducing mucus and other foreign material. Further benefits associated with this herb are observed in the heart muscle and heart rhythm because of the presence of potassium.

Following is an excellent program to remove cysts in fibrocystic breast disease (see glossary.)

Take 15-20 drops of Elderberry Extract 3-4 times daily along with 600 units Vitamin E once daily. Cut down on red meat and eliminate caffeine (coffee, tea, chocolate and cola drinks.) Increase estrogen supply by taking Siberian ginseng or MP. CAUTION: If symptoms of heart disease are present, see your doctor.

SUGGESTED USE: Begin using three drops in a cup of warm water; gradually increase to ten drops in a cup of water.

ANTI-SPASMODIC and NERVE TINCTURE

HERBS: ANTSP EXTRACT - Distilled water, alcohol, scullcap, valerian root, myrrh gum, black cohosh, cayenne and vegetable glycerine.

PHYSIOLOGIC ACTION: ANTSP helps in cases of cramps, convulsions, delirium, fainting, hysteria, and tremors.

SUGGESTED USE: Three to five drops two times daily.

BLOOD TONIC

HERBS: CAYENNE EXTRACT, Cayenne, alcohol.

PHYSIOLOGIC ACTION: Taken internally, cayenne improves blood circulation. Cayenne is a natural stimulant that serves as food for the heart.

Applied externally on bleeding wounds, it acts to stop bleeding. Helpful for colds, flu, headaches, nosebleeds and when rubbed on toothaches.

(Another liquid which will numb toothache pain is clove oil. It can be applied to the infected tooth and perhaps the gum.)

SUGGESTED USE: Add to warm water according to taste. For a

weakened heart, use care and gradually increase the dosage. A special diet and daily exercise are also suggested for heart disease.

CAUTION: If heart disease symptoms are present, see your doctor before using Cayenne Extract.

BURNS (Minor)

HERBS: COMFREY/DERMAID OINTMENT - Tallow, comfrey leaves, olive oil, beeswax and peppermint oil.

PHYSIOLOGIC ACTION: This ointment can be used for treatment of chapped skin, minor burns, sunburns, abrasions, scrapes, bruises and diaper rash.

SUGGESTED USE: Apply as needed for a soothing and skin softening effect.

HEMORRHOIDS

HERBS: MULLEIN/HEMRELIEF OINTMENT - Tallow, mullein leaves, peppermint oil, olive oil and beeswax.

PHYSIOLOGIC ACTION: This ointment helps relieve the burning, itching and discomfort associated with hemorrhoids and other minor skin irritations such as those due to contact with irritant plants (poison ivy, oak or sumac) or insect bites. It soothes dry, scaling skin and sunburns.

SUGGESTED USE: Apply externally as needed.

INSECT BITES

HERBS: PLANTAIN OINTMENT - Tallow, plantain leaves, peppermint oil, olive oil and beeswax.

PHYSIOLOGIC ACTION: This ointment helps to relieve the pain, swelling and itching of insect bites as well as stings, minor cuts and scrapes.

SUGGESTED USE: Apply externally as needed.

ITCH RELIEF

HERBS: CHICKWEED/X-ITCH OINTMENT - Tallow, chickweed, peppermint, olive oil, beeswax.

PHYSIOLOGIC ACTION: This ointment provides soothing relief from itching, pain and discomfort of hives and other minor skin irritations and rashes.

SUGGESTED USE: Apply externally as needed for a soothing, skin moisturizing effect.

NASAL CONGESTION

HERBS: NOSE/MENTHODYNE OINTMENT - Petroleum jelly, peppermint oil and spearmint oil.

PHYSIOLOGIC ACTION: This formula relieves cold distress including coughs, nasal congestion and the accompanying muscular aches and pains.

SUGGESTED USE: Apply ointment under nostrils and on the throat. In the cases of chest congestion, rub into the chest and back.

EQUILIBRIUM and EAR TINCTURE

HERBS: B&B EXTRACT - Distilled water, alcohol, black cohosh, blue cohosh, blue vervain, scullcap, echinacea and vegetable glycerine.

PHYSIOLOGIC ACTION: B&B Extract helps the body combat inner ear infections which sometimes cause hearing loss. It relieves symptoms of hysteria and nervous disability.

SUGGESTED USE: Take three to six drops orally.

The following program has been successfully used for partial deafness: 3 drops of B&B Extract followed by 3 drops of oil of garlic have been placed into the ear in the evening. The ear was sealed with cotton. This program was followed each evening for a week. On the seventh day the ear was washed out with a mixture of apple cider vinegar and distilled water (half & half.)

PAIN TINCTURE

HERBS: WILD LETTUCE AND VALERIAN EXTRACT - Distilled water, wild lettuce, valerian root, alcohol and vegetable glycerine.

PHYSIOLOGIC ACTION: This tincture calms nerves and relieves minor pain. Wild Lettuce and Valerian Extract is a natural sedative.

SUGGESTED USE: Take three to ten drops in warm water or add to an herb tea.

SKIN TINCTURE

HERBS: BLACK WALNUT EXTRACT - Distilled water, black walnut hulls, alcohol and vegetable glycerine.

PHYSIOLOGIC ACTION: High in organic iodine, this herb has proven effective in controlling external and internal parasites and cleansing toxic blood. It is useful against fungal infections such as ringworm and athlete's foot, as well as other scaling and itching. Black Walnut Extract may be used as a gargle for gum and mouth conditions.

SUGGESTED USE: Take three to six drops in hot water or in an herb tea. For fungal infections apply externally to affected area.

STOMACH TINCTURE (Colic)

HERBS: CATNIP & FENNEL EXTRACT - Distilled water, catnip, fennel seed, alcohol and vegetable glycerine.

PHYSIOLOGIC ACTION: This tincture works on minor spasms, acid stomach and gas. It also soothes indigestion and nerves and is excellent for colic. In colic, painful gas is sitting on the upper portion of the stomach. The catnip relaxes the stomach muscles and the fennel helps expel the gas.

SUGGESTED USE: An adult can take forty drops in a cup of water. If a colicky baby has twenty drops, it will usually be asleep within twenty minutes.

SYRUPS

Many times children and the elderly find it difficult to swallow capsules and tablets. In these cases, syrups and tinctures can be used very effectively. They can be added to small amounts of juice, water, and herb teas to make them more palatable.

When immediate results are needed, the liquid extracts are suitable because of their rapid absorption.

BLOOD CLEANSER SYRUP

HERBS: RED CLOVER COMBINATION - Honey, alcohol, red clover blossoms, chaparral, licorice root, peach bark, Oregon grape roots, echinacea, cascara sagrada bark, sarsaparilla root, prickly ash bark, burdock root, buckthorn bark, distilled water and vegetable glycerine.

PHYSIOLOGIC ACTION: This combination aids in cleansing the circulatory system. It is best suited for those who cannot assimilate raw plant fiber in dry herb form.

SUGGESTED USE: One teaspoonful with a glass of water or mix one teaspoonful in warm water for a tea. Drink before each meal or at least twice daily.

COLD AND FLU SYRUP

HERBS: ANT-PLG - Apple cider vinegar, vegetable glycerine, honey, garlic, comfrey, marshmallow, white oak, black walnut, mullein, scullcap, and gravel root.

PHYSIOLOGIC ACTION: Being a natural antibiotic, ANT-PLG helps prevent colds and flu. This combination is actually Dr. Christopher's famous anti-plague syrup.

SUGGESTED USE: One teaspoon 3 times daily or, as symptoms develop, may be increased up to one tablespoon every half hour. See the Diet section under "Cold Sheet Treatment" for a more complete description of the use of ANT-PLG.

HEART TONE SYRUP

HERBS: HAWTHORN BERRY SYRUP - Honey, hawthorn berries, alcohol, distilled water and vegetable glycerine.

PHYSIOLOGIC ACTION: Hawthorn berries help feed the heart to improve its action. (Also see Combination "H.")

SUGGESTED USE: One teaspoon twice daily. If symptoms of heart disease are present, see your doctor immediately!

PARASITE SYRUP

HERBS: VF SYRUP - Honey, alcohol, fennel seed, black walnut hulls, senna leaves, male fern, tansy, tame sage, wormwood, distilled water and vegetable glycerine.

PHYSIOLOGIC ACTION: VF will aid the body in the expulsion of internal parasites. It is most effective when incorporated with fasting and a cleansing diet.

SUGGESTED USE: Mix four drops in an herbal tea or juice three times daily or one teaspoon each morning and night for three days. On fourth day drink one cup of senna and peppermint tea. Rest two days and repeat two times.

GLOSSARY

ADAPTOGEN: An agent which balances and restores strength to a particular area of the body.

ADRENAL GLANDS: Two small glands which lie above each kidney and produce various types of hormones including adrenaline; aldosterone; cortisol; and some of the sex hormones, androgen, and progesterone. Illnesses associated with disorders in the hormone production of the adrenal glands include Addison's disease, Cushing's syndrome and pheochromocytoma.

ALTERATIVE: Agent which purifies the blood. Usually promotes cleansing action of the spleen, kidneys and liver. Generally should be used over a long period of time. Cancer, skin disease, arthritis and infections are partially caused by impure blood.

ANODYNE: Substance used to ease pain.

ANTHELMINTIC: Substance used to expel or destroy intestinal worms.

ANTACID: Substance which corrects acid conditions in stomach, bowels and blood.

ANTIBIOTIC: Substance which inhibits growth of and destroys bacteria.

ANTICATARRHAL: Substance which eliminates mucus condition.

ANTIEMETIC: Substance which relieves and suspends sickness of the stomach and thus prevents vomiting.

ANTIPYRETIC: Substance which cools the system and reduces fevers.

ANTISEPTIC: Substance which prevents the growth of bacteria.

APERIENT: Mild laxative.

APHRODISIACS: Substance used to increase sexual power or excitement.

AROMATIC: Herb which emits a fragrant smell and produces a pungent taste. Used mainly to make other medicines more palatable.

ASTRINGENT: Substance which causes tissue contraction.

BILE: An alkaline fluid produced by the liver. It has two functions: to help break down fats in food so that it can be absorbed and to neutralize the acidity of the stomach contents when they reach the duodenum.

CARDIAC: Substance which has an effect on the heart.

CARMINATIVES: Substance used to expel gas from the stomach, intestines or bowels.

CATHARTICS: Substances which cause evacuation from the bowels.

CELL PROLIFERANT: Substances which will help healthy cells grow faster when cell growth is required (Eg. after a wound, burn or broken bone.)

CHOLAGOGUE: Substance which promotes flow of bile.

DEMULCENTS: Substances used to relieve internal inflammations, provide a protective coating and allay irritation of the membranes.

DEOBSTRUENTS: Substances which remove obstructions.

DIAPHORETIC: Substance used to increase perspiration.

DISCUTIENT: Remedy that dissolves and removes tumors and abnormal growths.

DIURETIC: Agent that increases flow of urine.

EMETIC: Remedy that induces vomiting.

EMMENAGOGUE: Remedy that stimulates menstrual flow.

EMOLLIENT: Substance that softens and protects tissue.

ENZYMES: Chemical substances, produced by living cells, which speed up the rates of chemical change in our bodies.

ESTROGEN: Any of a group of chemically similar hormones that cause female sexual development. It is produced mainly by the ovaries, but also by the adrenal glands. Estrogens play an essential part in the hormonal control of menstruation. When the estrogen level becomes too low to stimulate the uterine lining, menstruation ceases and a woman is said to be in menopause.

EXPECTORANT: Agent that loosens or induces expulsion of phlegm of the mucous membrane of the nasal and bronchial passage.

FIBROCYSTIC BREAST DISEASE: The presence of one or more cysts in the breast, making the breast lumpy. They are serious because they may obscure the identification of other lumps in the breast including cancer.

GALACTAGOGUE: Agent that promotes secretion of breast milk.

HEMOSTATIC: Agent that arrests internal bleeding.

HEPATIC: Agent which strengthens, tones and stimulates secretive functions of the liver. Useful in the treatment of jaundice and hepatitis.

LAXATIVE: Agent that promotes bowel action.

LITHOTRIPTIC: Agent which dissolves and discharges urinary and gall bladder stones and gravel.

LYMPHATIC: Agent used to stimulate and cleanse lymphatic system.

MITOCHONDRIA: Tiny structures inside each body cell which produce almost all the energy a cell needs to live and function. Mitochondria deficient in CoQ10 are unable to efficiently convert food into energy even though sufficient food is present.

MUCILAGE: Substance with soothing quality for inflamed part of the body.

NERVINE: Substance which acts on the nervous system to temporarily relax nervous tension or excitement.

NUTRITIVE: Substance which supplies a substantial amount of nutrients to aid in building and toning the body.

OPTHALMIC: Agent used for healing diseases of the eye.

PARASITICIDE: Agent that kills and removes parasites from the skin.

PRECURSOR: Raw materials the body needs to build a substance it naturally requires. An example of this in herbal medicine is either sarsaparilla or APH. Both of them have the raw materials for the body to manufacture testosterone. When body builders take either of the above precursors, it starts a chain reaction which results in accelerated muscle growth. Thus, the results of taking APH or sarsaparilla are similar to the results of taking steroids but without the harmful side effects.

Another example is valerian. A sleeping pill will force the body to sleep. Valerian will help the body to produce sleep if sleep is required.

PURGATIVE: Agent which causes copious excretions from the bowels. More drastic than laxatives or aperients. For use only by adults.

SEDATIVE: Agent that relieves excitement of functional activities of a body part. It influences circulation thus reducing nervous expenditure.

STIMULANT: Agent that assists functional activity of the body and thereby increases energy.

STOMACHIC: Agent which gives strength and tone to the stomach.

STYPTIC: Agent which contracts tissues or blood vessels; used to check bleeding.

TONIC: Herb which increases energy and strengthens the body. Tonic herbs increase strength of nervous and muscular systems while improving digestion and assimilation.

VERMIFUGE: Substance which expels or destroys worms.

VULNERARY: Substances which promote healing of cuts, wounds and burns by stimulating cell growth and protecting against infections.

DIETS

A clean body will absorb herbal and other nutrients faster than one filled with mucus, toxins, poisons and other wastes. These diets help to cleanse the body. Then the herbal programs will be much more effective.

These diets should not be used for long periods of time nor by people in extremely weakened conditions or when serious healing crises arise. In such cases, people should avoid the diet until they are strong enough to handle it. If problems persist, they should seek professional medical advise or contact a natural health care practitioner.

After going off the diet, it may be a good idea to consume less red meat and eat more fiber and fresh fruits and vegetables. It may also be a good idea to occasionally go on a Primadophilus and liquid chlorophyll program to help maintain healthy intestinal flora.

THREE DAY CLEANSE

When the well-known herbalist and naturopath, Dr. John R. Christopher, used to go on his lecture tours, he would tell people about his famous purification program, the three day cleanse.

First thing in the morning, drink **two drinking glasses prune juice**. This is primarily to draw toxins from the body into the intestines. Within half an hour take **one glass apple juice**. Swish each mouthful thoroughly to mix with saliva.

An adult male should consume a **gallon of apple juice** throughout the day. If you must cheat and eat, have one or two apples per day. Take **1-2 tablespoons olive oil** daily to help lubricate bile and liver ducts, etc.

In case of constipation during this time, one can take **prune juice** and/or **Multilax #2** three times daily.

It is advisable to work up to and work down from the three day cleanse or any other fast by eating only light meals.

COLD SHEET TREATMENT

This is a program to clear up such infections as colds and influenza. It has even been used to eliminate cravings for alcohol, nicotine and other drugs.

This treatment works because germs cannot thrive in a healthy body. The germ is the scavenger that lives on mucus, toxins, poisons and filth. If you are a healthy person, your mouth may presently have germs of, say, chicken pox, tuberculosis and measles. But you do not have these diseases because the germs will not multiply in a body filled with nothing but healthy cells. But, if you are run down and full of toxins, watch out!

To begin the treatment, the patient may require a cool enema. This is the first step in removing filth from the body. In severe cases, this can be followed by a garlic enema (also called a "garlic injection.") This is a blend of apple cider vinegar, cold water and finely grated garlic. Use a pint for an adult and less for a child. Hold as long as possible before voiding. This way a maximum amount of garlic can be absorbed by the body.

At this point, drink one or two tablespoons of Dr. Christopher's anti-plague syrup (ANT-PLG.) Because of the strong garlic taste, it would be a good idea to chase down this natural antibiotic with a liquid such as grape juice.

A tablespoonful each of several diaphoretic herbs such as dry mustard, cayenne and ginger should be added to a bathtub of water as hot as the patient can stand. The patient should stay in the tub for around 15 minutes and drink a few cups of a diaphoretic tea. Yarrow tea can be used. Alternately, the patient can drink hot herbal tea or water with three or four capsules of **Herbal Composition.**
While sweating, the patient may get light headed. If so, place a cold washcloth on his forehead.

At the beginning of this treatment a natural fiber sheet such as flannel should have been placed in a deep freeze or ice water.

When the patient steps out of the bathtub, he should be wrapped in the cold sheet and tucked into bed with plenty of blankets. At this point, expect copious amount of perspiration to flow through the patient's pores. Let the patient sleep. If the patient took enough diaphoretic tea, the perspiration breaks loose old toxins, drugs, medicines, mucus and poisons which have accumulated over the months or perhaps even years.

After the patient awakes and the sweating is finished, he should be sponged down or showered. He can now satisfy his hunger pangs with vegetable or fruit juices.

LEMON AID CLEANSE

This diet is another one for eliminating toxins. At the same time it revitalizes the body. Normally no food or supplements are taken during the lemon aid cleanse.

The diet consists mainly of drinking 6-12 large glasses of this mixture daily:

> 2 tablespoons lemon juice
> 1 tablespoon maple syrup
> 1/10 teaspoon cayenne pepper
> Water to fill glass

To make up a day's supply, mix:

> 2 cups lemon juice
> 1 cup maple syrup
> 1 or more teaspoons cayenne

Mix 3 tablespoons in each large glass of water.

To help rid the body of toxins, one can have an enema and/or alternately take two **Multilax #2** three times daily.

Someone who has been on this cleanse for a week or more should come off it very slowly. The digestive juices can be stimulated the first day by drinking a mixture of half water and half orange juice (preferably freshly squeezed.) Broth from cooked vegetables is a good second day choice. Then a person can slowly ease back onto solid food.

BODY REBUILDING

After an illness, a body can be toxic and malnourished. It is therefore wise to rebuild the body at this time.

The digestive system will most likely be suffering. **Primadophilus** will increase the number of "friendly" bacteria in the intestines.

Siberian ginseng will build up the strength in the body. After regaining strength, a cleansing program will help prevent future viral diseases. If **Red Clover Combination** or **CS** are a part of this cleanse, they will help remove toxins from the blood stream.

As well as using the correct herbal aids, it is important to watch the diet at this time. Eat fresh wholesome foods and avoid overly-processed foods.

If someone feels that he has more than his share of colds and other viral diseases, he could probably solve the problem by going on a "low-mucus diet." Health food stores have entire books written on the subject.

Basically, the idea is to eat more revitalizing foods and minimize the mucus-forming foods. The mucus-forming foods include eggs, milk products and (this is the important one) highly refined flour products. These foods will form mucus in which the viruses will thrive. The revitalizing foods include fruits and vegetables (raw when possible,) grains, nuts and seeds.

ARTHRITIS CLEANSE

Stiff joints become flexible and pain is reduced when people follow this program. Expect it to take two weeks before you begin to see results.

Mix up the following cleansing broth daily:

>   2 lb. potatoes -- clean, diced, NOT peeled
>   2-3 cloves garlic -- diced   One quarter cup parsley
>   3-4 stalks celery -- diced   2-3 quarts water

Bring to a boil and then simmer slowly for one and a half hours. Set aside to cool. Separate liquid from the pulp. The pulp can be thrown away.

Drink the cleansing broth whenever desired. Take one capsule of Yucca-AR twice daily (and build up to two capsules three times daily over the next two weeks.)
During the cleanse stay away from citrus fruit, red meats and milk.

CAUTION: This cleanse clears uric acid and other toxins from the system.

During the first day and maybe even the second, expect to have diarrhea as the toxins are leaving your body. So, it is best to start this program when you can plan to stay home the next day.

BIBLIOGRAPHY

Johnson,E.S., Kadam,N.P., Hylands,D.W., Hylands,P.J., **Efficacy of Feverfew as Prophylactic Treatment of Migraine,** British Medical Journal, Vol.29, 1985

Santillo, Humbart, **Natural Healing with Herbs,** Hohm Press, Prescott Valley, Arizona, 1985

Malstrom, Dr. Stan, **Own Your Own Body,** Community Press, 6th Printing, Orem, Utah, 1977

Murray, Dr. Michael, **Nutritional Information on Silymarin,** Kirkland, Washington

Christopher, Dr. John R., **Childhood Diseases,** Christopher Publications, Springville, Utah, 1978

Aikman, Lonnelle, **Nature's Healing Arts,** National Geographic Society, Washington, D.C., 1977

Stuart, Malcolm, **The Encyclopedia of Herbs and Herbalism,** Orbis Publishing Limited, London, England, 1979

Mills, Simon, **The Dictionary of Modern Herbalism,** Lothian Publishing Company Pty. Ltd., Melbourne, Australia, 1985

Jensen, Dr. Bernard, **Chlorella Jewel of the East, The Nutrition and Dietary Consultant, June, 1986**

Willard, Terry, Feeling Good with Natural Remedies, Wild Rose College of Natural Healing Ltd., Calgary, Canada, 1984

Bergner, Paul, **Ginkgo Biloba, An Herb for the Ailments of the Old Age,** Alive Magazine, July, 1988

Zeleny, Robert O., **The World Book Medical Encyclopedia,** Chicago, Il, 1988

INDEX

A-P 37
Acidophilus 28
Acne 39, 40
Activated charcoal 5
Adrenal glands 32, 16, 22
Aging 30
AKN 39
Alcohol abuse 34
Alfa-Max 5
Alfalfa 5
Allergy 22
Aloelax 34
Alterative 9
Amoebic dysentery 13
Anemia 21
Angina pectoris 15
Anorexia 7
ANT-PLG 47, 54
Anti-plague 47
Antibiotics 9, 28, 42, 47
Antihistamine 22
Antioxidant 9, 34
ANTSP 43
APH 32
Arteries, inflammation of 13
Arthritis 5, 8, 11, 21, 23
Arthritis diet 56
Aspirin 20
Assimilation 35
Asthma 17, 22
Astralagus 5
Athlete's foot 46

B F&C 25
B F&C Ointment 25
B/P 24

B&B Extract 45
Bacteria 22, 28
Bad breath 10, 17
Barbiturates 19
Barley grass 5
Bayberry 6
Bee pollen 6
Beet powder 6
Bile 17, 20, 23, 35
Black cohosh 7
Black walnut 6
Bladder 7
Bladders, ulcerated 20
Bleeding 9, 43
Blessed thistle 7
Blood cells, white 11
Blood circulation 43
Blood Cleanser 24
Blood clotting. 23
Blood detoxifier 8
Blood platelet 23
Blood poisoning, 11
Blood pressure 12, 22, 24
Blood purifier 7, 11, 18
Blood sugar 32, 38
Bloodstream, detoxifying 10, 39
Body, rebuilding 56
Boils 40
Bones, broken 10, 25
Bowels 35
Bowels, inflammation of 6
Brain 14, 36
Breath, bad 28
Breathe-Aid 39
Breathing 22, 27g

BRE 39
Bronchial passages 12
Bronchitis 27
Buchu 7
Burdock 7, 23
Burns, minor 44
Bursitis 23
Butcher's broom 8

C&F 27
Calcium, 26
Calm-Aid 37
Candida albicans 22, 41
Caprinex 41
Carbuncles 11, 40
Cascara sagrada 8
Cataracts 29
Catnip 8
Catnip & Fennel Extract 46
Cayenne 9, 43
Cayenne-Garlic 24
Cell proliferator 10
Chamomile 9
Change-o-Life 36
Chaparral 9
Chest congestion 45
Chickweed Ointment 45
Childbirth after-pains 37
Childbirth, ease in 18
Chlorella 10
Chlorophyll 5, 10
Cholecystitis 11
Cholesterol 12, 17, 24, 31
Circulation 9, 24, 31
Cirrhosis 11, 34
Clove oil 43
Cold sores 28
Colds 10, 13, 27, 32, 45, 47, 54
Colic 8, 12, 46

Comfrey 10
Comfrey Ointment 44
Congestion, Nasal 45
Conjunctivitis 12
Constipation 8, 34
Contraceptives 36
Convulsions 43
CoQ10 30
Cortisone 16
Coughs 27, 45
Cramps 36, 43
Cranberry 10
CS 24
Cuts 25, 44
Cystitis 7 , 15, 20
Cysts 43

Damiana 11
Dandelion 11
Deafness 45
Deodorant 5
Derm-aid 44
Dermatitis 40
Detoxification 25
Devil's claw 11
Diabetes 38
Diaper rash 25, 44
Diarrhea 18, 19
Dieting 41
Digestion 13, 17, 28, 35
Digestive aid 23
Diuretic 7, 28
Dizziness 13
Dropsy 11, 17
Dysentery 19

E-Z-Sleep 33
Earaches 13, 42
Ears, infections in 31

Ears, ringing in 13
Echinacea 11
Eczema 8, 9, 11, 18
Elderberry extract 42
Emmenagogue 7
Endocrine glands 12, 19
Energizer 29
Energy 6, 29, 30
Enzymes 5
Epilepsy 19
Equilibrium 45
Estrogen 7, 20
Ex-Stress 37
Eyebright 12, 29
Eyesight, weakness of 12

Fatigue 14, 29
FC 36
FEM-CAL 26
Fem-Mend 36
Fennel 12
Fenu-Comf 27
Fenu-Thyme 30
Fenugreek 12
Fever 20, 27
Feverfew 12
Fibresyl 18
Fibrocystic breast disease 43
Flu 27, 30, 47
Flu, prevention of 11
Fo-ti 12
Free radical 34
Frostbite 25
Fu-Sho 31
Fungi 22, 41

Galactagogue 7
Gall bladder 16, 20, 35
Garlic 12

Garlic & Parsley 33
Garlic, odor controlled 22
Garlic, Oil of 42
Garlicin 22
Gas 5, 10, 12, 13, 46
Gastritis. 10
Germanium 20
Germs 54
Ginger 13
Ginkgo 13
Ginseng Gotu Kola 29
Ginseng, Siberian 14
GL 30
Glands 30
Golden seal 14
Gotu Kola 14
Gout 8, 11, 15, 23
Guar gum 14

H Combination 31
Halitosis 28
HAS 22
Hawthorn 15, 48
Hay fever 22
Headaches 31, 37
Hearing 13, 45
Heart 9, 15, 24, 31, 43, 44, 48
Heart attacks 23
Heavy metals, 10
Hemorrhage 9, 17, 20
Hemorrhoids 8, 44
Hepatitis 16, 34
Herbal Composition 27
Herbal eyebright 29
Herbal Mineral 40
Herbal Slim 41
Herbal Up 29
Herpes simplex 28

Hiatus hernia 16
HIGL 32
Hives 45
Hormone balance 33, 36
Hormone, female 19
Horsetail 15
Hot flashes 36
Hoxey 25
Hydrochloric acid 17
Hypoglycemia 16, 32

IF 33
Illness, recuperating 56
IM-AID 32
Immune system 5, 6, 10, 32
Impotence 32
Indigestion 13, 46
Infections 11, 12, 30, 32, 33, 42
Infections, glandular 31
Infections, inner ear 45
Inflammation 16
Influenza 27, 54
Inner ear 45
Insect bites 44
Insomnia 15, 33
Insulin 38
Intestinal floral 28
Iodine 16
Iron 21
Itching 45

Jaundice, 11
Juniper berry 15

Kava kava 15
KB-2 28
Kelp 16
Kidney 10, 15, 17
Kidney stones 15, 16, 17, 20

Kidneys 16, 33

Laxative 8, 17, 19, 34
Lemon Aid Cleanse 55
LG 35
Licorice 16
Ligaments 25
Liver 9, 16, 20, 34, 35
Liver, detoxifying 10
Liver, enlargement of 11
Liveron 35
Low-mucus diet 56
Lower Bowel Cleanser 35
Lungs 27
Lymph nodes 30, 33

Marshmallow 16
Memory 13, 36
Menopause 36
Menstrual cramps 7
Menstruation 36
Mental functions 36
Menthodyne 45
Metabolism 16, 40
Migraines 12
Milk thistle 16, 34
Milk, mothers' 7
Minerals, trace 40
Mitochondria 30
MK-9 40
Morning sickness 13
Mosquito bite 31
Motion Mate 37
Motion sickness 13, 37
MP 36
Mucus 12, 27, 30, 43
Mucus membrane 14, 17
Multilax #1 34
Multilax #2 35

Multilax #3 34
Mumps 31
Muscles, sore 31
Myrrh 17
Myrrh-Golden Seal Plus 41

Naturalax #1 34
Naturalax #2 35
Naturalax #3 34
Nausea 13, 37
Nephritis, 7, 20
Nerve tonics 20
Nervous system 15, 19, 37
Nervousness 15
Nettle 17
Nose Ointment 45

Oat fiber 17
Osteoarthritis 23

Pain 20, 37, 46
Pancreas 32, 38
Parasites 6, 38, 46, 48
Parsley 17
PC 38
Peristaltic muscles 35
Pimples 39
PK 38
Poison ivy 44
Poisons 5, 34
Potassium 11, 43
PR 39
Premenstrual cramps 7
Primadophilus 28
Prostate 39
Pruritus 40
Psoriasis 18, 34
Psyllium 17

Radioactivity 16
Rashes 45
Red Clover 18
Red Clover Combination 47
Red raspberry 18
REMEM 36
Reproductive system 11
Respiratory tract 39
Rheum-aid 23
Rheumatism 8, 11, 21, 23
Ringworm 6, 46
RNA 10

Salmonella 28
Sarsaparilla 19
Sciatica 8
Scullcap 19
Sedative 20, 46
Senility 13
Senna 19
SEN 36
Sexual functions,
strengthening 32, 33
Sexual stimulant 11
Shock 9
Silent Night 33
Silymarin 16, 34
Sinus 22
SKC 41
Skin irritations 45
Sleep 19, 33
Sodium alginate 16
Sodium caprylate 41
Sore Throat 31
Spleen 11, 33, 38
Sprains 25
Stamina 6, 14, 29
Staph 28
Steroid abuse 34

Steroids 19, 32
Stings 44
Stomach, upset 27, 31
Strep 28
Stress 14, 20, 22, 29, 32, 33, 37
Strokes 23
Suma 19
Sunburns 25, 44

T Combination 40
Teeth, abscesses of 11
Teething 26
Tension 37
Testosterone 19, 32
Thisilyn 16, 34
Three Day Cleanse 53
Thyroid 16, 40
Tonsillitis 11
Toothaches 43
Toxins, eliminating 55
Tumors, 20

Ulcers 10, 17, 41
Ureteral infections 15
Urethra 7
Urethritis 20
Uric acid 11
Urinary passages 16
Urinary system 15
Urination, difficulty in 17
Urine, bloody 10, 20
Uterus 18
Uterus, prolapsed 39
Uva ursi 20

Valerian 20
Valium 19
Varicose veins 8
Veins 8

VF SYRUP 48
Viruses 12, 22
Vision 13
Vitality 14

Weight control 14, 41
White oak 20
White willow 20
Wild Lettuce and Valerian 46
Worms 38
Wounds, healing of 10

X-Itch 45

Yeast 22, 28, 41
Yellow dock 20
Yellow Dock Formula 38
Yucca-Ar 23
Yucca 21